POST-ATOMIC GLOSSARIES

Antony Owen was raised in the working-class heartland of Coventry which alongside growing up in Cold War Britain influenced his poetry on conflict. His work features in UK School lesson resources for peace education by CND and Quakers. He is a recipient of the Museum of Military Medicine Award (2018), The Bread & Roses Award and most notably was shortlisted for The Ted Hughes Award for new work in poetry for his study of atomic bomb survivors taken in Japan.

Also by Antony Owen

The Battle	(Knives Forks and Spoons Press, 2022)
Phoenix	(Thelem Press, 2021)
Cov Kids	(Knives Forks and Spoons Press, 2020)
The Unknown Civilian	(Knives Forks and Spoons Press, 2020)
The Nagasaki Elder	(V. Press, 2017)
Margaret Thatcher's Museum	(Hesterglock Press, 2015)
The Year I Loved England [w/ Joseph Horgan]	(Pighog Press, 2014)
The Dreaded Boy	(Pighog Press, 2011)
My Father's Eyes Were Blue	(Heaventree Press, 2009)

Post-Atomic Glossaries:
New & Selected Poems

Antony Owen

Broken Sleep Books

For Dylan Hockley

© 2024 Antony Owen. All rights reserved; no part of this book may be reproduced by any means without the publisher's permission.

ISBN: 978-1-916938-29-8

The author has asserted their right to be identified as the author of this Work in accordance with the Copyright, Designs and Patents Act 1988

Cover designed by Aaron Kent

Edited and Typeset by Aaron Kent

Broken Sleep Books Ltd
PO BOX 102
Llandysul
SA44 9BG

CONTENTS

POST-ATOMIC GLOSSARIES

SON OF THE MUSHROOM CLOUD	11
THE LAST HIBAKUSHA	12
THE MEDICAL EXAMINATION OF AN ATOMIC BOMB SURVIVOR	13
SOAP FOR AN UPSETTING SHADOW	14
CASTLE BRAVO	15
THE LAST HOUSE OF HIROSHIMA	16
桜 BLOSSOMS	17
DEAR MR OPPENHEIMER	18
NAGASAKI SILENCE	19
CHILDREN OF LITTLE BOY	20
AN ATOMIC BOMB SURVIVOR DONATES HER BODY FOR SCIENTIFIC RESEARCH	21
JAPANESE BONES	22
FROM ASHES	23
DEVIL	24
THE LAST MINUTES OF HIROSHIMA MARKET	25
REQUIEM FOR ENOLA GAY	26
AFTER THE MUSHROOM CLOUDS	27
MIDNIGHT IN HIROSHIMA PEACE PARK	28
STARBUCKS ON SKULLS	29
NUCLEAR LAKE	30
OPERATION MOSAIC	31
OFFICERS MESS	32
PHANTOM	33
A BLACK SOLDIER MEETS HIS MAKER IN THE SNOW	34
IF THE END COMES	35
AMERICAN CHOCOLATE	36
THE CHOICE	37
IF WE TOOK A DRIVE OVER EARTH NOW	38
THE JOY	39
KYOUFU (FEAR)	40

A LEADING POET TOLD ME TO END MY SUITE OF POEMS WITH HOPE	41
FRANKENSTEIN IN THE HOLY LAND	42
I AM WITNESSING A LIVESTREAMED GENOCIDE	43
DOOMTOWN	44
WHO ONLY KNOW THE PHEROMONE OF KIN	45
I AM A BLACK HOLE	46
POST-ATOMIC HAIKUS	47

THE BATTLE

MAN UP	53
SEXUAL FEELINGS	54
ADULT AUTISM	55
MONSTER	56
I PUT A SPARROW OUT OF HER MISERY	57

COV KIDS

MEMOIRS OF JOB SEEKER 328509B	61
KERESLEY GIRL	62
CYRILLE REGIS	63
MY NAN WAS A COV KID WHO DIED DREAMING	64
THE HOUSE THREE DOORS FROM MY NAN'S	65
LOVE IN THE AGE OF LOCKDOWN	66

PHOENIX

A GERMAN CIVILIAN QUIETLY CONTEMPLATES HER BLITZED CITY	69
POSTMAN IN THE SMOKE	70
INFERNO	71
ESCAPING SOBIBOR	72
THE INTERROGATION OF A WOMAN RESISTANCE FIGHTER	73
HOW TO FIND THE FALKLAND ISLANDS	74
COVENTRIEREN	75

THE UNKNOWN CIVILIAN

A GERMAN SOLDIER IN RUSSIAN BOOTS	79

IMAGINING WILFRED OWEN'S 104TH BIRTHDAY	80
A SYRIAN SLAM POET DIES WITH HER MOUTH OPEN	81
A BLACK NURSE TENDS TO WOUNDS	82
FLIGHT 93	83
SIKH SOLDIER	84
THE SUICIDE OF PRIVATE JOHN DOE	86
FOR SYRIAN BOYS WHO WILL NEVER KISS A WOMAN	87
RWANDA	88
THE UNFASHIONABLE DEATH OF ANOTHER SYRIAN DAUGHTER	89
DEAD BABES STOLEN FOR NUCLEAR TESTS	90
LETTERS OF LAST RESORT	91
BELFAST ON WEATHER REPORTS	92
43RD BIRTHDAY	93
BAGHDAD ZOO	94
SREBRENICA MASSACRE	95
THE MATHEMATICS OF PEACE	96
A KOREAN SOLDIER IS BLOWN IN HALF	97
ASTRONAUTS	98

THE NAGASAKI ELDER

THE LAST FARE COLLECTOR OF HIROSHIMA	101
PEARL HARBOUR	102
THE NAGASAKI ELDER	103
GREEN TOMATO	104
BLACK RAIN	105
PURPLE CHALK	106
TO FEED A NAGASAKI STARLING	107
FAT MAN	109
SKETCHING OF AN ATOMIC HORSE	110
THE FERRYMAN	111
THE ART OF WAR (I)	112
A PARK NEAR CHERNOBYL	113
HOW TO SURVIVE A NUCLEAR WINTER	114

MARGARET THATCHER'S MUSEUM

KIM KARDASHIAN BROKE THE INTERNET	117
FERRIES	118
THE COLD WAR	119
NIGEL FARAGE STREET	120
THE OTHER IRON LADY	121

THE YEAR I LOVED ENGLAND

THE DREAMER OF SAMUEL VALE HOUSE	125
COVENTRY STREET	126
THE YEAR I LOVED ENGLAND	127
THE BURNING OF NUMBER EIGHT'S WHEELIE BIN	128
THE LITTLE THINGS DESTROY US	129
FAUN	131
LOGO	132
VERMIN	133
THE SHELF STACKER	134

THE DREADED BOY

MEDUSA	137
THE SCENT OF A SON	138
PENDANT	139
EGGS	140
THE QUIET NIGHTS OF WAR	141
DIAMONDS	142

MY FATHER'S EYES WERE BLUE

FOXGLOVES	145
THE SPIDER AND THE WIFE	146
THE COPPER MAN	147

ACKNOWLEDGEMENTS	149

POST-ATOMIC GLOSSARIES

NEW POEMS

A lot of rumours circulated back then that the hibakusha (atomic bomb survivors) were carriers of serious diseases or that if two survivors got married, they would have disabled children
— Koichi Wada

SON OF THE MUSHROOM CLOUD

In weeks they will check you for lice
ask you to bleed again for America
unsheathe your foreskin for milk
shine a light into your periscope eyes.

In that soot-saggy sky
through a flesh and blood cosmos
you flew twenty meters into hell
through will-o'-the-wisps of souls.

You said these were the lucky ones.
Zombies marched to the river mouth.
their brown eyes like conkers on string
the clogged up river swallowed them.

The swollen sun broke its violet seal
revealing only mountains and monsters.
When it rains clear you stand in it
to feel your parents explode upon you.

THE LAST HIBAKUSHA
After Sueko

I see her bent from old age
the archipelago of her spine
aglow in zombified light of long dead stars.

This night she will obey her rituals
recalling her face in black puddles
how atomic rain turned the river mauve.

I see her fireball tattoos in cling film
mercurochrome fusing the keloids
a dragon slayer of shedding skin.

When the last Hibakusha dies
curled wick-like into her oils
I hope they bury her facing the stars.

THE MEDICAL EXAMINATION OF AN ATOMIC BOMB SURVIVOR

> *The Atomic Bomb Casualty Commission (ABCC) developed a poor reputation among the Japanese population. The military-led US atomic bomb investigation team—the predecessor of the civilian ABCC had sent all their data and pathology specimens from Japanese casualties back to Washington, rather than keeping their findings in Japan.*
> — The Lancet

In your body's post atomic glossary
your gums were the inland sea
receding with the insulted sun
to Earth's pale sister oh so shy.

Today you take a sheaf of your hair
the perruquier was busier than ever
he assessed the coarseness and hue
"This hair is Korean" he insisted.

They have lollipops at the clinic
elders warned of beautiful ogres
who invited children to the jar
then jam-jarred their organs for Washington.

You have no teeth yet you spoke
and sometimes you can taste metal
it reminds you of air before black rain,
it reminds you of first stage leukaemia.

You have no hate for America
you have no love for America
and the world is deaf you said,
I am nothing but a shell revealed then reclaimed.

SOAP FOR AN UPSETTING SHADOW

Trace her scarred estuaries,
these old atomic birthmarks
dredged an orphan from woman.
Her linen of skin a cat o nine tails
she walked to volcanoes of corpses,
encountering ghosts glued to their shadows.

Trace her stained-glass eyes.
She is a cathedral of wounds,
gallows of gamma rays ignited her,
"I was a lamp in the human darkness,"
she would permit these words annually.
They insisted she scrub an upsetting shadow.

In new Hiroshima, her grandchild plays Baseball.
In old Hiroshima she is permanently Japanese.

CASTLE BRAVO

> *On March 1, 1954, the United States exploded a hydrogen bomb, codename Bravo. At 15 megatons, Bravo was a thousand times more powerful than the bomb dropped on Hiroshima. Both Bikini and Enewetak's native islanders were evacuated from their island homes prior to the nuclear tests, hoping to avoid radioactive fallout. But, the inhabitants of Rongelap 150 kilometres away were not so fortunate.*
> — Greenpeace

Where blizzards never fell
a white powder smothered atolls
and all the children ate the tepid snow.

The crowned distant beast
shapeshifted against earths sac.
God herself witnessed what man had created.

There was a mutilated sun
no longer distant as before
coconut crabs led the exodus.

Patriotism doesn't exist on Rongelap
Just threads of blood from women's frocks.
Another miscarriage of life, of injustice.

THE LAST HOUSE OF HIROSHIMA

Your old face was parchment.
A thousand lines of shallow graves
to a smooth clearing the firestorm left.

That hill of human eyes you whispered of
the dead wept in gamma strobe rainbows
It was just moisture leaving their bodies you said.

Afloat in your waters your son would be perfect.
You counted the steppingstones of her toes
waiting for her at the shore of warm milk.

Some mothers gave birth to smoke and silence.
The chapel was known as the oath room.
The toes of Jesus faded from kisses.

All the survivors of Hiroshima are fading away
like shadows of people permanently cast
black flames of a blacker rain.

桜 BLOSSOMS

> *The pumpkin field in front of the house was blown clean. Nothing was left of the whole thick crop, except that in place of the pumpkins there was a woman's head"*
> — Fujie Urata Matsumoto

After sky died inside out
Moon was a weeping Geisha
her face only revealed weeks later.

Some trees perished in acts of wisdom
gifting their seeds in armorial sap
Some emerged defiant into blossoms.

When water fuses to the low-lands
and survivors watch burns turn to rock
only then do they welcome monsoons.

The trees of Nagasaki and Hiroshima
were shrines of hope in the early days
if they could prevail so could the ghosts.

DEAR MR OPPENHEIMER

Beneath your crafted nebula
I picture your dead noon walk
casting a long shadow eastward.

In the post atomic abendrot
you brush off Alamogordo sand
like glitter from a forbidden kiss.

Dear Mr Oppenheimer,
sky is badged in yellow stars,
magenta stars, violet dust.

Dear Mr Oppenheimer,
this night your star was born
sunset bled over Hiroshima.

At the IMAX film of your life
a man scoffs bulb warm Dorito's
sharing his awe on TikTok –
the new age Brittanica.

NAGASAKI SILENCE

> *I was found with my belt buckle thrust into my stomach and my skin blowing from my cuticles.*
> — Firestorm survivor

In that bloated star
bells hung their black tongues
stretched in a mid-drip drool of melt.
They pulled away arms from ragged railings.
Doilies of skin peeled away a fine purpled silk.

Meet me at the brow of human hills —
time has frozen here in the bleak banshee.
Cicadas excite the static ground of eyes and bone.
It is eternally two minutes past eleven in the morning.
An old lady wets her lesions and glows like a new demon.

Sea turns frigate grey.
Americans came for a new star.
Everyone's skin is hanging in stripes.
This child is a prisoner of war and nations.
He is blind yet witnessed the whole world, and hell.

CHILDREN OF LITTLE BOY

> *The atomic bomb that destroyed Hiroshima was named "Little Boy" and was 29 inches long. This bomb detonated 580 meters above the ground with a heat burst stronger than our sun. The weapon destroyed or severely damaged two thirds of all of the buildings in Hiroshima. Today, the total number of nuclear weapons exceeds 12,000 which is more than the entire cities of the world with a population of 100,000 or more.*
> — Sources: ICAN, Yale, Britannica

Sadako,

your hair upsets the foul zephyr

it comes out in clumps blowing to America.

Sadako,

You have yellowed your bedsheets again

take them to the rivers that swallowed Hiroshima.

Doctor,

soon Sadako will fold as the last paper crane

be sure to cut her cherry blossoms with Japanese steel.

Doctor,

Sadako's blood is like Muleta from a Matadors hand

abloom in water draping death in the emperor's scorched clothes.

Emperor,

Presidents, people who are ants above the magma,

listen to your blood-fire and tell yourself you are stars and mortal.

AN ATOMIC BOMB SURVIVOR DONATES HER BODY FOR SCIENTIFIC RESEARCH

I am just the silk of a nervous system
its vast tree fanning in a storm of creation
and all the nests have long gone of song
If you bring me an American cuckoo
then I will throw my doves.

I was just a girl who bled into a woman.
A Japanese shape in a polka dot dress,
the pattern branded onto my skin.
Each circle my ground zero.
Each burn your firestorm,
so here is your body.

JAPANESE BONES

> *Those who drank water after the Pikadon (atomic bomb) died instantly from the heat*
> — Hibakusha

In post atomic November
when wind was still as Nagasaki shadows
you looked at your face in the rivers warped water
threw a stone at yourself so you could disappear there.

In post atomic December
it was warm as American smiles
cold as speculums of Japanese steel.
Your bloodline ended in the menstrual dusk
a new day was born but not your rush wrapped son.

You wrote about Japanese bones,
how they protruded from atomic darkness like lilies.
Every now and then they stay with you all summer.
You remember a child holding a huge ear in black rain,
when he drank and died there, bubbles burst from his eyes.

FROM ASHES

In the post atomic borealis
sun rose deformed in magnesium pillars.
The atom-cumuli sent trained horses around in circles.

These eggshell bones did not want to leave there.
Two shapes were glued together into plasticine.
Leave them frozen from fire in a final union.

As months passed into Hiroshima months
I read of a flutist converting atoms into music.
Every dawn at 8.15 she always stopped abruptly.

As years passed by, survivors became a stain.
Nobody wanted to grow a flower in the ashes,
and yet they arrived, their children playing flutes.

DEVIL

> *After the atom bomb destroyed my city, nobody wanted to have children with women who survived*
> — Hibakusha

Nobody talks about the black waterfalls,
rivers of hair cascading into a torrent
eyes bulging into mushroom clouds,

If only they resembled Marilyn Monroe
naked as a beautiful flame
we'd gather at the fires?

Imagine Sun dangling like the devil's locket
heavy from forty thousand faces
an aurora borealis of blood.

At the tea ceremony a survivor drifted away
she half peeled an orange and handed me the rind
"My skin came off like this" she said.

THE LAST MINUTES OF HIROSHIMA MARKET
I still hate the glow of the setting sun
  — Emiko Okada

You recalled the last minutes of Hiroshima market
how sugared locusts spangled in the emperor's sun
until his new clothes hung as skin from fingernails.

You and your daughter made rice balls the old way,
too many sunflower seeds would split apart the grains
you scolded her for this in softly spoken wisdom.

Aflame in your uterus a babe would scroll your skin
its palm fanning warm waters where he arrived silent,
still as koi in black ponds of bludgeoned palaces.

You recalled cantaloupe rinds aglow on black souls.
Anything was moisture would be consumed and
anything with moisture would consume them in return.

For seventy years you kept the rice-ball your daughter made,
freckled in seaweed from the mouth of old Hiroshima.
Its waters cool your feet each cruel August sun.

REQUIEM FOR ENOLA GAY

The shunned sky retreated.
A blistered eye burst across the blue.
Godfearing man elected Satan and his dreaded egg.

They named it Little Boy
hunchbacked into the troposphere, he rose.
His dreamcoat of flesh and bone dragged across sky.

Thirty years later in Texas
on an airfield strip they recreated Hiroshima
they sold toffee apples in the shape of the bombings.

AFTER THE MUSHROOM CLOUDS

For weeks birds flew blind
and then dawn was silent
they swept up sparrows
into plump black bags
burnt them in craters
with fish by the sea.

On the flat scorched corn
lambs still as cirrus
waited for wolves.
They arrived thin
unable to eat,
laid down
the wild
in them
gone.

MIDNIGHT IN HIROSHIMA PEACE PARK

For Hideko on her 66th Birthday.

I sat on the cold Hiroshima grass.
Bugs popped to dust on the UV light,
and I thought of your sister in fiery squalls.

It is beautiful here at midnight in Hiroshima.
A throng of shadows brush the Genbaku
like a beautiful stranger that got away.

I see a Japanese boy in a baseball shirt,
he lives the Asian-American dream.
Once a year he bows to Oleanders.

STARBUCKS ON SKULLS

Rain hushed the cicadas
bivouacked amongst souls they emerged
turning sky into a black rain of blemished bass.
Every now and then ghosts remind this city of its sick star.

Moon is paler here, loose as a button hanging by a thread
resembling an eyeball dangling from a ghost of skin.
Beneath us are old warped Hiroshima gates
I can hear them through the nymphs.

I am drinking my Americano in the emperor's old clothes
American and Japanese logos engulf darkness.
Down the road the baseball stadium is full,
cultures mix like Wasabi and hot dogs.

Once upon a time in this very spot at Starbucks Hiroshima
a scimitar flame cut through homes and spirits
and in mornings after the dreaded black car
orphans folded into wax-white cranes.

NUCLEAR LAKE

For Karipbek Kuyukov

Between 1949 and 1989, the Semipalatinsk Test Site was one of the primary locations for Soviet above and below ground nuclear testing. The first Soviet nuclear weapons test, codenamed Pervaya molniya or First Lightning, took place at Semipalatinsk on 29 August 1949. In total, 456 nuclear tests, including 340 underground and 116 atmospheric tests, were conducted at Semipalatinsk Test Site facilities.
— Nuclear Threat Initiative

Born below tortured sunrises
atoms made three hundred and forty lakes
and before rain filled them Kazakhstan was moonscape.

Your organs were little easels visible through your skin
in time you saw yourself as a living canvass
you painted the crimes with toes and Ox hair.

When cattle drank from Uranium lakes
in time wind would strip them of fur
people scraped their tongues, and their babies would be still.

They once dragged two lovers from a lake
its neon beauty invited their virgin bones.
They glowed like the foetuses in formaldehyde museums.

OPERATION MOSAIC
> *Imagine being a soldier in the army present at a nuclear test, wearing just a uniform of shorts, a shirt and a hat and being told, 'turn your back to the blast and push your palms into your eye sockets'*
> — Frank Walker

On the condemned beach
sixty-eight-year-old footprints remain
fish scaled tiles adorn abandoned homes.

A crab pink sign curls on a breached fence
tiny bones shale the craters outer rim
a scorpion hangs from a Union Jack.

You can only stay one hour here
before your soul scrolls your skin to leave
like the turtle shell cleaved from the blast.

A nuclear test veteran wrote he craved milk,
he drank so much of it and never knew why.
I have never seen cancer so hungry.

OFFICERS MESS

You answered my question of what war is —
it's the smell of army issue soap in stolen Afghan water —
how blood rushes to the drain like sperm at deaths egg
the baby in a bag with rusks and wires got there I hope, you said.

You told me of the officer's mess and made a popping sound.
"I remember the roof raining with brain matter and hate,
blood smells like burning wires and eggs but its more than that
it's a fucking life do you get it? "It's a son and you know nothing."

You told me to look at the ghost with the boyband smile and gas-blue eyes.
"That pretty boy skewered a man's eye out with his bare thumbs"!
"There is no why" you said and that humans never go on leave once soldiers.
You mocked my choice of drink and told me that whiskey is a decent burial.

It's been eleven years and I heard you went to find yourself in Ibiza.
I heard you just stepped off the twenty first floor like sky would hold you.
By six am the next morning they had hosed your blood into the overfill
It left an unsightly stain on the patio, they replaced it with a new one.

PHANTOM

The cruellest ghouls wear white sheets
They awake yelling in confusion
racing through hospital wards
Then looking at their legs
and they're lying in bed
two stumps in gauze.
a sobbing mother
a fidgeting father,
a lowly civilian,
a trophied man,
the awkward
phantom
haunting
himself.

A BLACK SOLDIER MEETS HIS MAKER IN THE SNOW
After Roy McFarlane

His black fist abloom
like a blackbird in a hard gale
cartwheeling into moons cold spasm.

Learn from the narcotic owl
of lowly beasts burrowed in warrens
soldiers and rats in cycles of servitude.

In prayer-page pits they were lowered
further from heaven fastened
black men jettisoned with lye.

IF THE END COMES

If the siren murders birdsong
I shall take my daughter to the park
Watch her learn to climb into the sky
and tell her she will grow big and strong
then I'll carve our names into stubborn bark
waiting until we become atoms and eternally fly.

I would not want to see her flesh blow like silk
To watch her blue eyes eclipse into milk.
I'd rather be part of her world than ours
The black stems of nuclear sunflowers
Yes, I'd rather leave this world mortal
What is death but just another portal?

Come my beloved wife let us walk hand in hand
Lift our daughter through fields they banned
This land is ours for fifteen minutes or so
Before the winds of fire shall blow
This sky to the end was kind see
Here it comes, stand behind me.

AMERICAN CHOCOLATE

On leave you kept returning to the stills of war
giving out Hershey bars to Afghan children
sweet wrappers lighting up the dust
one caught in the gaunt thicket.

An entourage is a tell-tale ghost of disturbed earth,
in the mountains it will cause men to be demons.
They shall come and find the sweet wrappers.
They will line up children with brown lips.

A rainbow of birds emerging from the avifauna is an omen.
Something has alarmed them like fired lightning.
How many days flow in these blood red streams?
What names are returning to paradise?

On leave you kept returning to the Hershey wrapper,
still in the thicket catching the soured wind.
It is these images that made you leave us.
Your pendulum bones hanging from a belt.

THE CHOICE
    After Wahid Rahimdil

This old wind —
a pallbearer of nationless breaths — *Pashto, Dari,*
you can feel a sickness of the ancient soil accepting young bones.

In Afghanistan
you can watch a pink cloud of plump mosquitoes.
Hear the anthem of the nationless from a restless bass of bodies.

Sky turns Soviet red
it is hard to know drones from American stars.
Those aliens have invaded us yet we are invisible, nationless.

Show me an American Eagle
for all we have seen are drones and vultures
and vultures' queue around carrion in hierarchical lines.

When Afghanistan was born
I like to think that a wild horse bolted from a barn
dragged its keeper who tried to break him with cruelty.

Come and see what a drone does.
Watch wigwams of bone and Hyde from my elders.
This is how the nationless become after the eagle leaves.

Come and watch our choices —
forced displacement and wind slicing discarded Quran's
most of the people had nothing but Calais or Paradise.

IF WE TOOK A DRIVE OVER EARTH NOW

I dreamt you and I were driving over Earth's sky and tuned into the radio of each country hearing ballads fading out to white noise. We noticed moon was a frosted bullet-hole and behind the black glass of space was the explosion of impact where brain matters of Gods making new worlds were actually reflecting the end of ours. We passed the blue desert of ocean to ice and watched it shrink like snowflakes in greenhouses. We turned up the radio over Syria and all of the stars turned to cats-eyes taking us to streets of roadkill in human clothes. As we broke down their sun hurled itself through this street in an act of self-immolation for all the people maddened by war. I dreamt you and I were driving in darkness with earth and moon as our busted headlights, "it's no wonder we got lost" *you said.* We turned off the radio and watched sap bleed out from elms as sparrows gave it song. We slept in the beautiful earth.

THE JOY
        After Raymond Antrobus' *'With birds you're never lonely'*

For four hundred years your Sequoia circled sky
a marriage of wood and stars until the glitch.
The fiery sore that cleaved you open.
An etched heart and arrow,
names in penknife kanji.

Survivors circle trees now,
like Nagasaki streetcars on inertia.
The passengers burnt where they stood,
a passage of static lifting their hair like fans,
married to atoms they chanted names to Yeshua.

A man once wrote of the joy.
He saw a black rain of starlings over the sea,
his boat drifted into the nothingness and listed,
that moment he smiled so wide his gums bled burgundy.
The joy he felt lifted like the burn skin of his bride to be.

The joy
are screams ending
like stretched silk rending.

The joy
are survivors gekkering
their hearts carved in lettering.

The joy
are Hibakusha giving,
all the lost life to all of the living.

KYOUFU (FEAR)

She loved him
Radiation can be beautiful
His hands flat against her scars
As if they were lotus flowers at sunset
Dusk turns everything into oil on canvas.

He loved her
Even when she disappeared
her eyes fixed at jet scarred skies
waiting for a dot to fall and blind her
waiting for the streetcar to call her parents' names.

They hated August,
watching Hiroshima Park
and Americans fanning themselves
eating ice cream trying to keep cool
dropping litter wrappers above her brethren

A LEADING POET TOLD ME TO END MY SUITE OF POEMS WITH HOPE

For the Nagasaki schoolgirl spatchcocked by fire
I shall not disrupt her blast punctured eyes
And end my suite of poems with hope.

For prisoners of war imprisoned in memorials stalag
I shall not light a candle in the begging myth house
And ask ghost authored gods for faux peace.

For the shaved Parisian woman who kissed a (Ger)man
I shall not insult their tongues forbidden to touch
And remember her not covering her vagina.

A leading poet told me to end my suite of poems with hope.
I said I do not shape or edit my stanzas for awards
Like the Parisian woman they shall not be shorn.

Hope can be found in the apothecary of rebel poems —
A Refusal to Mourn the Death, by Fire, of a Child in London
and to end my poem with the fire inside Dylan Thomas

FRANKENSTEIN IN THE HOLY LAND

There is a place near Bethlehem
where children twist alum keys for water
drinking from radiators to survive
and my children, your piss reeks of bonfires
your eyes have almost switched off.
There is a place we've never heard of
Where an old woman planted flower seeds
Into the pocket of a forced invader
Yelling when you fall dead flowers will grow
Through eye sockets of your devil's skull.

I AM WITNESSING A LIVESTREAMED GENOCIDE

Sky
in heavens eyes
sun knows no ceasefire
it unthreads from the heavens
and again I grieve for yellowy stars.

Stars
you are yester-lights
so long to have arrived
like all of the named limbs
let fathers wash them whispering Jannah.

Child
take our debts
do not blockade prayer
we do not deserve your counsel
you are too heavy for the heavens to carry.

Brothers
and sisters
take my pallor
paint it onto the paled
if only we never offended what made life itself.

DOOMTOWN

Yellow throats of marigolds surrounded the bomb
Below the sacred ground mannequins with Chanel smiles
They never blink like desert's glaucoma eye.

At night the mountains resemble children sleeping foetal shaped
a whipsnake coils around a gopher next to a gutted Cadillac
the mannequins are placed around a table with turkey and trimmings.

All for caged pigs it is silent in Doomtown this evening
One of them squeals as if to know of fires to come
The stoned goat's jaws are jellied from gnawing wire.

In a millisecond the pink of the pigs is hurled to the ether,
Momma mannequin bloats into a wax plate by the turkey
Her bottom half remains immaculately dressed.

The goat horns fall into heart shapes and they found a bell.
The all-American daughter's arm was found twirling a baton.
The father drinking coffee from the window was not to be found.

Hours later a sparrowhawk died in the gamma-mauve sky
Its beautiful explosion was not felt miles from there
A scorpion in its maddening drew slow circles in sand.

On television they never showed the lack of glory,
Hazel Bishop cosmetics interrupted the bleakness
Offering the same nail varnish that even survives firestorms.

WHO ONLY KNOW THE PHEROMONE OF KIN

In Gaza just as it did in Hiroshima
a flower cracks stone from its will
a mother sidles her legs to bury sons
a father cuts his throat with the murdering stone
his loved ones stem the wound and he lives.
This week the moon is closest to Venus
This week I am closer to this uninhabitable planet.
This week a ring of light encircles the moon
It is light refracting from the crushing atmosphere.

I AM A BLACK HOLE

After Paul Williams

I saw a yellow finch today
its colour ran clean away
a ghost of Coventry grey.

I saw an ambulance today,
the blue of its siren cleaved its way
past a murdered church of progress and clay

I watched a robin on my sill.
the burn of her breast brought a chill
my goosebumps formed a skin of twill.

I watched my eyes form to stones.
left my paralysis, oared my bones
abdicated kingship of broken thrones.

I felt the loss of atmospheres
she was my world whose end nears
and leaves me stuck from the weight of our years.

POST-ATOMIC HAIKUS

For Ellis Brooks

AUGUST 5TH 8.15A.M
Wind catches her frock
throwing cotton sunflowers
into a strangers hand.

FLESH
Half peeled mandarin,
warm torn skin, dimpled, fragrant
cloud vapours consumed.

FLASH
Flashlight fishermen —
tessellated nets stretching,
Koi carp flicker shockwaves.

IMPRINT
Epidermis dress,
strapless patterned skin, wearing
August's bleak tattoo.

PITH
Blood warm fruits unfurl.
Keloids strafing altered skin,
wars bled mosaic.

WRECKAGES
River mouth whispers –
harbour these bone lantern ships,
moored upon wastelands.

NAGASAKI
Fat man awakens,
devouring breath, birdsong sky.
Skeleton city.

AFTERWARDS
September vista –
amputated bridges cling
shadows unshackled.

TEARS
Wounded eyes hold sun,
raindrops of remembrance scorch.
Hiroshima falls.

PEACE
Doves crumple skyline.
Egg shells throb syrupy life,
dry white blossoms rain.

RESURRECTION
Watercolours spring —
bees sip Nagasaki dust,
lotuses explode.

HOPE
Aogiri pilgrims
share rings betrothed to sun
old roots blossom hope.

CITYSCAPE
Dominoe city
night falls around dark matter,
windows glow like stars.

In Hiroshima
she folded into origami
paper face burning.

In Hiroshima
sons kissed Mothers through oiled lint
writhing like silkworms.

In Miyajima
blind deer washed up pink
clawing bleached rocks.

Victorious fly
this bony perch of caged man
leave his velvet heart.

emaciated crow
bursting with mockery and song
hopping on icecaps.

HAIKU (I)
Hiroshima sleeps
shadows of Hackberry trees
stroke foetal children.

HAIKU (II)
Wind catches her frock
throwing cotton sunflowers
onto lover's hands.

HAIKU (III)
Papier mâché boy
tears burn us all briefly
yours set God ablaze.

HAIKU (IV)
Doomtown mannequin
your all-American smile
facing blown off limbs

THE BATTLE

KNIVES FORKS AND SPOONS PRESS (2022)

75% of all UK suicides are men
— National Office of Statistics

MAN UP

In the guillotine of stratus
nights head dropped bloody
and I thought of my friend hanging.

My boss said he's worried about me
how everyone else has seen it too
he sent me a gif to remind me I'm only human.

My friend died in a ropes eye
she loved horses so an apt departure
her neck galloping in horsehair.

My boss told me it's been three weeks
that it's time to man up and hit target.
I told him I'm only human to his face.

SEXUAL FEELINGS

I touch-screened endless categories to feel something
couldn't find lovers just Milf and Anal.
I have no sexual feelings.

I have no feelings.
The dark sides of daily moons I swallow
are anti-depressant, anti-human.

This level of honesty is not to be encouraged, is it?
Someone will say I am oversharing.
Jill from HR will be in touch.

What is touch anyway?

ADULT AUTISM

Before I was special
I was an angel in formaldehyde.
I was a minotaur with bulging bollocks.
I was Perseus versus Medusa trapping her in my shield.

Now I am special
I am a jar of pickles prickling the palate.
I am a Roman statue the Visigoths defaced,
its penis severed, dusting the pink roses vulva.

MONSTER

My doctor is wearing a mask.
I am removing all of mine,
to reveal who I am
the muted worker
the vocal rebel
a fading boy.

I just called my lockdown Doctor
she prescribes me potions.
I swallow pills of rain
gulp government air
and citalopram.
I'm a chemical
Frankenstein.

I PUT A SPARROW OUT OF HER MISERY

My cat broke the wing of a sparrow.
It flew into boomerang curves
arriving back to its talon.

I put a sparrow out of her misery
it flew kited with its intestines —
bunting for a cold creator.

COV KIDS

KNIVES FORKS AND SPOONS PRESS (2021)

MEMOIRS OF JOB SEEKER 328509B

I awake drowning in the landfill of first light,
each day gets heavier as I try to carry them quietly but fail.
Yesterday I stared at an application form and two hours passed,
I'd written a statement of who they want me to be and guess I drifted away.

What makes a grown man curl up like a foetus?
When he's reborn from the cunt of a job centre's door and given a zone to die.
What makes a grown man get smaller each day?
is when yawning boys at agencies roll apps and eyes at disappearing people.

I want to report my tragic disappearance,
It happened again this morning when my wife wept in secret to protect me.
Every morning she puts on a brave face and feeds the black dog and elephant.
Her body aches from work and dragging the iron chains of her shadow slave.

The truth of unemployment is the greatest lie you believed –
a chav with eight children from ten different Mothers can be possible,
the migrant who robbed that job and food from an Englishman's mouth.
No, the truth of unemployment is how quick it eats a person's mind.

The truth of unemployment is the sea of ash the lost awake in.
Some feel the only thing they can control is not life but the other,
like that bloke from Sunderland who Dave659 shared on twitter,
and that woman outside Poundland at the end of her tether,
telling me her life meant nothing, that she felt, like nothing,
that she was nothing and how she could find nothing.

I had to do something,
and tell you.

KERESLEY GIRL

Once upon a time in the ghost-town grey we kissed and
it was softer than the boxers fist I taped before he was knocked out
yeah, you knocked me out in round one and here we still are
fighting life.

Something about Keresley girls that makes the Cov boys melt —
remember how snowflakes felt on your lips the first time?
It's okay to melt from a kiss made with such love.

The thing with Cov girls is that they come from a blitz,
we are made to melt upon their pale hearths of skin
it is a safe place, a dangerous place, *but your place.*

The thing with Cov girls
is that they'll share a kebab with ya,
they will share an Uber with ya and maybe their bed
but if you cross em they will end you with a glance.

CYRILLE REGIS

Guiana born you learnt how to charge through bananas like mist,
those slave-lands were your anchor to run and live free
I picture a leather ball as your chair beneath sunsets.

In West Bromwich you learnt from shoelaces the smell of England,
the puree of banana, saliva and the soiled chalk of white men,
you shrugged them off like an own goal to decency.

You were the uncaged magpie, a song against the bulldog's snarl,
more than a black man, but a human who silenced the noise,
the smiling tower on bedroom walls of proud black boys.

In Coventry came a magpie, a sky-blue heart in a city Thatcher greyed,
you charged through the right wing to Kop-song murmuration's
Each time you played win or lose was an unknown celebration.

In Liverpool you became a liver-bird with a frond of the Magpies blue,
monsters made monkey noises but you never walked alone,
they took you in like bird-song, like one of their own.

Your first England cap when they posted you cowardice in a bullet and ink,
"If you put your foot on Wembley turf, you'll get one for your knees".
How sweet the grass of England and the black defiant rose.

Guiana born, you learnt your first steps charging through the foggy flora,
the best pass your father made was from your mother at birth,
he must have felt he'd won, that ball of life now returned to earth.

MY NAN WAS A COV KID WHO DIED DREAMING

I was four when I saw my Nan lying dead in foetal position delivered in her sleep to the primordial skin of sky. My Mum tapped at the window with her blue hairy breath shrivelling like a dead violet on the window, We three brothers sat in our duffel coats sobbing because our Mum was and because we knew death was all about the colour blue. Flesh blue, Veins blue, Breath's blue, The policeman blue, Daimler blue, Siren's blue, Mother blue, Our tongues after a slush puppy blue. My Mother's Mother was the kind of woman who could turn a tin of spam into a meal for six and could stretch a spud from Monday to Thursday with breadcrumbs the birds never got to see. I remember my Mothers Father-in-law holding my Mum without their bodies coming into contact and when he said "God" my Mum turned the windscreen wipers on for no reason and then Tony Blackburn up full volume because my Mum loved her mum and absolutely hated Tony Blackburn, *except then, he was God.*

THE HOUSE THREE DOORS FROM MY NAN'S
> *Cov kids have a fire in them and that comes from the blitz.*
> — Coventry Evacuee

In the loft three doors from my Nan's a bomb fell over Joyce
the father crawled out holding his severed hand,
a woman told him to cover his privates
he was talking shock gibberish.

In the exposed pantry the torn lungs of gas pipes gargled,
someone commented on how nice the wallpaper was.
A dog snapped at the burst water mains barking,
then the question was asked *"Where's Joyce"?*

The nosey parker didn't want to look and got her Ted
he found a blanched ball of bones swaying on a beam
"I've found her" he yelled *"Poor old cow"*
"don't fuckin come in here" he pleaded.

My Nan was unscathed, just pinioned like a shrew in a cat's paw,
she was a driver of three carriages who wailed without stopping.
Maggie, Victor, Patricia; all of my kin staring into exposed houses
asking why does it smell of eggs and fish on the turn.

LOVE IN THE AGE OF LOCKDOWN

In Valencia,
Thin birds return to the barrio
an old lady who knows this silence ties nuts from her balcony
this is her act of love for birdsong, for the marshes they bring to her.

In Brittany,
a rich man's Gite is broken into
two weeks in August, they will never know it was a fox
she went there because barbarians dug up her den as her kits slept.

In London Zoo,
Wolves excite the silent air
then soda lights ignite and steal the full moon from them.
It matters not for a poet heard the cry and captured it to free them.

In Baghdad,
a widow lets her husband fly,
the colour of his eyes thrown to wind
nothing is said but she is grateful for the plague *it is not like war.*

Near Leamington,
a pigeon smashed into my wing mirror
it was just like a dirty angel had died in its own rain.
I went to pick it up, but a magpie came to drink from its heart and I let it.

In Guantanamo Bay,
they cannot stop the scent of white mariposa,
it enters the cells and makes the prisoners smile —
the pharmacist, the soldier, the carpenter, the erased.

PHOENIX

THELEM PRESS (2021)

A GERMAN CIVILIAN QUIETLY CONTEMPLATES HER BLITZED CITY
For Rainer

She is translating the Hamburg canvas of Lancaster, Halifax, Wellington and Stirling. The greys of homes guttural from gasps of backdraft breaths blowing out bed springs and bones that connected to flesh and labelled from the war machine the artist and Fuhrer painted lands over. She has seen a canary cage with only claws on the perch and a song and flight lost somewhere in the baroque cumuli. She is translating the Elbe twisting like a Corn Snake shedding its orange skin in the blood-orange dawn. Sun is ulcerous, it lays on the curving head of sky like curious Zeus disgusted at the acts of war. She is walking to the U-boat pen to see if her lover is part of the human rainbow hanging over Hamburg like a bridge to the yellow stars. His brother is there in his place and no translation is needed. Her foundations collapse.

POSTMAN IN THE SMOKE
For Margaret & Vic

In the smoldering amnion of new Coventry,
a singed dog dragged to water on its arse
licks the old nails deeper into his spleen.

A postman stands in the flame-grey postcode,
staring at doorways with chimneys around them,
moaning as they open to charred occupants.

The King is stuttering from the news —
a different stutter almost Germanic,
and Churchill will orate through smoke:
Dresden,
Hamburg,
Empire,
Martha's house.

INFERNO
After "Wunde" by August Stramm

In Dresden
it would be a crime not to touch
wicks of fingers pointing to God,
and take gold rings engraved with their names.

Identify them.
These dead firemen's buckets filled
with initialed rings weigh heavy.

In safe rooms
flames are planned by warmongers;
the rousing speech on still tables fat with ham.

Identify them.
These men who pin faceless kings to ghosts
and tell them they did what needed to be done.

In Dresden
it is a crime not to observe silence,
to not marry yourself to the past,
to be sorry for what happened here
and there
and there
and there
and.

ESCAPING SOBIBOR

For the 300 escapees and 50 who survived Sobibor extermination camp

I picture you watching a sunflower climb over the fence
its neck bowing to constellations of the wolf eye wood
did it give you ideas that all fences can bend from enough weight?

Why are people entering showers with their arms up to God?
a rumour escaped like sunflowers that it's to cram our kin in
nobody knows why the howling stops suddenly like wolves.

I picture the haggard-heavy face of a young German truck driver
hands spill out the tarp like vines of violets purpled from the pull
you can tell he was a handsome boy before the Eagle stole him.

I have a happy ending of three hundred sunflowers that lit up darkness.
An escapee of Sobibor tends to each one like new-born babes in a nursery,
she nurtures each seed and tells them they are yellow stars and shall live.

I have a happy ending that when she died those sunflowers thrived.
They flourished in packs like wolves and became intertwined like moonlight.
I have a happily ever after but it's frail as violets relying on light to reveal
them.

THE INTERROGATION OF A WOMAN RESISTANCE FIGHTER

You asked the interrogator to remove his gloves as he beat you to Bach
—
"Let us be skin on skin like you are on your dry wife
let my temple hurt the quaking flower of your fist —
be a man and finish me off, bound."

You told the interrogator that no number of teeth on the floor will matter.
"These are not my tongue that ties secrets to my deathbed
these are not my words that read lullabies to my son
these are just molars, incisors, red and white stones".

You asked the interrogator if his cock was hard when he removes your nails.
You tell him that this is the only time he can make only wet of woman,
that his gloves are held together by the hair of gassed Jews
that his time will soon be up and he will beg for mercy.

You decided the very moment of your passing
he never once was in control, not once.
Woman resistance fighter of Nimes
a school on your unmarked grave.

HOW TO FIND THE FALKLAND ISLANDS

You carry yourself like peat in Port Stanley air.
The authorial eye writes a hundred facial lines.
These are the new trenches frozen under fire.

Have you ever seen a field of wool and knitted limbs?
It's not how many dies but how they die over in the mind.
All my friends say so much, yet they say nothing.

I have something to say but will keep it locked.
Do you know why winds of war are made of black dots?
It is flies who sing above the reeking fallen, *glory be.*

Ken left no note, I get that he was already gone.
He moved like an Argentinian tango under fire.
A scripted rejection in the Job Centre killed him.

We used to laugh at penguins falling over as jets went overhead.
They would look at the unnatural as far as their heads bent back.
It was the weight that took them over, I know that weight well.

Ken told me to fuck off when I tried to dig in him.
Mad as a budgerigar forced to see himself in your cage.
Your fucking cage that made us dress pretty for glory.

You are all blind.
I go eyes wide open
with moon and sun.

COVENTRIEREN
> *(A word introduced after the Coventry Blitz into the German language meaning 'to completely destroy a city from the air'.)*

I heard unspoken communions made
which old people keep until death beds.
The wine of your wounds on bomb-glow breasts
exposed by *Luftwaffe* and a deep-rooted shame
you had to admit before guilt and cancer ate you.

If only you had laid him three yards to the left,
you would both be arm in arm down *High Street* now.
Mother and son in a beautiful chain of events
that began in the blitz and ended in your crib.
This never happened because you fed him on time.

THE UNKNOWN CIVILIAN

KNIVES FORKS AND SPOONS PRESS (2019)

A GERMAN SOLDIER IN RUSSIAN BOOTS
After Max Hastings & Willy Reese

Comrade, your thigh meat tasted like game and leather.
I needed your boots, so hung you over a fire to loosen them.
Your winters are so cold that my piss comes out like red fire.

Comrade, your eyes have thawed and it looks like you're crying.
Wolves are lapping the chummed snow and I feel nothing.
I am tame to them; their numbers expand like gun-metal.

Comrade, did you know old German newspapers blow all over Russia?
They come from trench-coats of Fuhrer's phantoms.
Your winter shall win you this war come summer.

It's so cold that I shot the oil from a panzer and made myself a skin.
My crimes are safe behind my perfect sky-blue eyes.
Aryan boys die like dogs, live white as statues.

Comrade, I defiled your body because I needed your boots.
I hacked into the ice with my blade like you were meat,
and you were meat, you were my footsteps home.

It's so typical that I am to die beneath the Soviet sickle moon.
My cause of death — a toe that slowly gnawed my left leg.
Comrade, the motherland is full of brothers in arms.

IMAGINING WILFRED OWEN'S 104ᵀᴴ BIRTHDAY

If you lived to see the maddened lions
would you say a few words to camera four,
and shake the hand of a corporate sponsor,
then read half of a poem before cutting to a break?

I'd love to see your mother's milk in your cataracts
well up where no man should stay in the eternal eye.
I'd love to hear you use the old term "shell-shock"
and Kay Burley from Sky apologise to the viewers for it.

If you lived to meet Keith from Rochdale back from Basra,
would you recognise that Keith from Rochdale is missing?
Would you let him say the C-word without shunning him?
Could Keith find his way home through deep red valleys on his wrists?

I'd love to see Boris Johnson take a selfie of you both by the lions,
and you'd say to him "Did you get shot at dawn dancing on my grave?"
I'd love to see you drunk in a wheelchair being pushed by Keith,
and the red of Keith's poppy, and the red of his piss bag on wire.

I'd love to see you alive in the encore of your "Anthem for Doomed Youth".

A SYRIAN SLAM POET DIES WITH HER MOUTH OPEN

Just weeks ago,
a Syrian slam poet screamed stanzas under her breath,
she knows how Kalashnikovs sound
like her father rat-a-tatting her door,
that night when she French-kissed a forbidden boy.

A Syrian poet lived with her mouth open,
that first time she read aloud Rumi
her breath dissolved bluing a window,
she touched herself into a woman *to let the girl go.*

Just seconds ago,
she performed her poem to the tomahawk sky,
these are not real tomahawks for they would scalp the top of the world
remove the brain and see that its swirls are the very fingerprints of God herself.

She screamed to the sky *"I am woman, a goddess of the shooting star"*
"The trebuchet light that swirls into sycamore to be one with earth"
"To be" ...

A BLACK NURSE TENDS TO WOUNDS

By morning the dead turn bottle-green,
pouring their vapors back to the reborn sun.
We do not tell the dying that the Lord never sent his sign.
I shall tell you of the crow and mockingbird that war made unnatural.

Last night I heard a mockingbird mimic the cries across the plateau.
I heard a nickering horse and the sound a tree makes when it dies.
Today I was watching a crow steal lint and viscera from a man,
last week he placed a name in my ear, so heavy it felt.

By dusk I rub gin beneath my nostrils and pray,
there once was a hymn my mother sang that healed me.
In Dominica it was the west wind cleaned by the tears of Jesus;
she told me as a child that if I hurt, I should let the Lord in to heal me.

Last week the colours ran from war, Ceylon to Coventry, black to white.
With bloodstained khaki, we turned the horse troughs carmine.
The bandy-legged nags took their bodies to a lime trench,
all of their bones shall be white and grow as red opiates.

I should mention that I am a black nurse in white man's world of war.
My hardest battle is tending to a wound that keeps reappearing,
there was a boy that would not leave my eyes as he went,
"You're an Angel" he said. My wings were black, broken.

FLIGHT 93

> *He wanted me to recite the Lord's Prayer with him. And he did. He recited the Lord's Prayer from start to finish.*
> — Mrs Jefferson, regarding passenger Todd Beamer.

In our first moments we arrive in motherships.
they sever the belt she had fastened around us
and we are hijacked into earth weeping for peace.
I like to think we leave in the same way, *but no.*

In final moments we become otherworldly.
We recite the Lord's prayer with a stranger.
Words become safeguarded sacraments.
"Tell my wife I love her. *She'll know* but tell her"

In final moments a spork can be a wooden spear.
A lowly office worker can be a gladiator, a shield.
When black clouds billow into our blue-sky town *we'll know.*
Let them see corn cover our tomb, no names please.

Last night I took a moment to think of old America.
My mind filled with smoke and I read the Lord's prayer.
I trespassed my lips on to the face of my wife and I thought,
she will forgive me for my failings as she smiles before seriousness.

SIKH SOLDIER

> *Britain did not fight the second world war, the British empire did.*
> — Yasmin Khan, (Author of *The Raj at War*)

We had a chance to unravel their turbans in winter breaths,
your stories are hidden in the stoic geriatric —
he is locked in eyes dementia blue,
it is too late now erstwhile friend.
Chime the bedpan it is time
float like stalled spitfires,
it is too late now and
breathe blue turbans
watch them unravel.
It is too late now
had our chance;
Singh, Lion,
brave hero
fearful of
the foe —
death
go
.

We had a chance to write a poem shaped in saluting chevrons,
your great grandson unearthed you in itchy khaki.
He is locked in your life, eyes wide and blue.
It is never too late when eyes burn tatters
they are immaculate in memoriam.
Men never look happy as soldiers
they strut into instructed death,
the truth is not unexpected,

a mosquito killed him.
Hokkaido nights are
darker than urine
no water here,
no humanity,
no England,
just land
just war,
just man
unjust.

3.8 million British Indian soldiers served in World War I & II as well as many others enlisted under the British Empire. Thousands of these soldiers were also Muslims – gakkar, awan, pashtunwani, jag, Mughal including warrior races of the Punjab.
— Sources: BBC, British Army Museum, The Spectator, The Independent and J. Mahmood.

THE SUICIDE OF PRIVATE JOHN DOE

I wonder in those brief Pay Pal unions
of credit card wanks and smileys
if hotgirl97 misses you at all.

I wonder if Ray got home after mourning you
those twenty-two days of hard whiskey,
fighting to be heard by headless suits.

I wonder if Bob at Wickes saw the rope
as he scanned it through and thought
that aint pulling no tree down.

I wonder which random thing that set you off,
was it Afzal in Texaco holding your tenner to the sun,
or a cherry short on a scratch card?

Pam in Tesco told Babs at the checkout
that she heard you were found all blue and that
whilst a man hung a lamb for the world to see.

I heard your Ma tell your sister in her belly
that heroes are ghosts of cold sons
born grey on the sleeves of a stonemason.

At least, that's what she means in those silences
when thumbnail faces of soldiers come home
in televisions and rope whilst Pam whispers loudly of loss.

FOR SYRIAN BOYS WHO WILL NEVER KISS A WOMAN

When tornadoes come
clouds roll tightly like judicial wigs and
war maddened children stare blankly into space
their heads are gavels metering out unseen sentences.

Up there in dreadful totems
climb flesh and bone of descendants.
An abacus of crows bicker from telegraph poles
communicating remnants of meat that whispered tenderly.

When little people die
their bodies are blue watercolours —
an art of war painted by those without ears
who sell their masterpieces only to those who bid the highest.

Where little people lived,
meats shone like red lamps on market day
and skinny dogs lapped blood in the cobbles
where Mukesh Junior learnt the music of trading.

In the parliament of slow kissing
I told my wife I love her and all the reasons why.
I told her for Mukesh who might not know a woman's lips,
and I told her for myself because at my most simple I am elegant.

> *An unprecedented 65.6 million people around the world have been forced from home by conflict and persecution at the end of 2016. Among them are nearly 22.5 million refugees, over half of whom are under the age of 18.*
> — **United Nations (2017)**

RWANDA

After Andrea Mbarushimana

A headscarf twitches on the wire
I am very interested in how it got there,
like shoes of different sizes strewn across a field
I am very interested in these states of man, *unlike America.*

A Toyota headlamp pops out with wires like a torn-out eye,
I am very interested in webs of smashed in windscreens
and how yellow dust of airbags spray like daffodils
blowing pollen into a human face, eyes open.

I am very interested in these things but do not say "genocide"
unless it is nine eleven or painted white like Van Gogh lilies.

THE UNFASHIONABLE DEATH OF ANOTHER SYRIAN DAUGHTER

Knock-kneed from Sarin she walked in perfect ovals
the girl is being evacuated from her bowels,
forget that image think of her an hour ago —

her fingers were jade from ripping coriander for soup,
she combed that smell into her mother's balding head
in fifty-eight minutes, the whole world will care.

A pilot from Earth once described the explosion of a bomb,
he said it looked like a folded-up Christmas tree
down there are people unwrapping their skin.

Back to the girl, or do we skip forward to the end? *"Yes, let's."*
Captain America and Wonder Woman from Tel Aviv came
they saved them all and the camera zoomed in on the credits.

Daughter of Syria played by a caption of *Coco* by *Chanel,*
Mother of Daughter interrupted by an advert for *Amazon,*
I travelled there last night to order some cologne, *how progressive.*

The end of this poem is random, imagine street dogs sharing meat,
they tear each other to shreds then another dog comes and another.
Leave an emoji at the grave, share the meat, shine a bat-light to Aleppo.

DEAD BABES STOLEN FOR NUCLEAR TESTS

> *Media reports have said 6,000 dead babies were snatched from hospitals in Australia, Britain, Canada, Hong Kong, the United States and South America for over 15 years without parental consent, and shipped to America for atomic tests.*
> — CNN, June 2001

No one came for your bones but a gloved hand.

I picture crab-red roads leading to sea as moon peels its violet skin.

No one came for your fossils so I excavate you,

I picture a mother who once had dreams empty as a derelict crib.

Skeletons are merely roots growing in ghosts or their haunted houses,

no one came to ask permission to take your bones,

no one brushed around sand burned to blue glass.

I picture a red birthmark of hell expand into the regurgitated winds.

I am collecting your bones and laying them in a poem.

You would be old now and yet you will always be young and ancient.

A poet in Oxford is writing a poem about the smell of Wordsworth's cottage,

so, I came for your bones and the weight for one is too much to bear.

I am collecting your bones and I am tired but dare not rest.

Last night I learnt that babies hear songs whilst rowing in uterine

so yes, I am collecting your bones from the nuclear fires,

I will bury you here in the seed of a poem's full stop.

LETTERS OF LAST RESORT
For Rebecca
According to the 2008 nuclear war documentary The Human Button (featured on BBC Radio 4), there were four known options given to the Prime Minister to include in the letters of last resort. The Prime Minister instructs the submarine commander to: 1) retaliation 2) non-retaliation 3) using own judgement 4) place submarine under the command of another Allied country such as Australia or USA.

I picture her writing the letters of last resort,

scratching a tomb in her best handwriting, in all her finery.

I picture her as that woman from Hiroshima, skin like cheap rags

but she would be safe in the bowels of beautiful Earth sipping fair-trade tea.

I picture the worst, a submarine commander yelling London yet she is mute.

What if he had a family there and, in that moment, felt a maddening fire

I picture the atonement on a girl from Moscow, a girl of the womb

you will be unmade by a man who clips his toenails in bed.

I picture a blue Hiroshima sky, the blueprint of God,

she carried this green seed drenched in her water.

Autumn leaves were her letters of last resort

I read them once and heard them whisper.

I picture the best, a submarine commander clipping his toenails in bed,

he is watching *The Blue Planet* shaking his head at a dying Polar bear,

the bobbing ice mimics his final breaths starved of food,

that submarine commander weeps, *there is hope yet?*

BELFAST ON WEATHER REPORTS
> *They have nothing in their whole imperial arsenal that can break the spirit of one Irishman who doesn't want to be broken.*
> — Bobby Sands

I was eight years old when I first truly saw Ireland
Michael Fish stuck sunshine over Belfast and it fell off,
they got the weather wrong that week for it rained there.

I was eight years old when I first truly saw England,
humans smeared a dirty protest over prison walls
rib-cages and iron bars served the same purpose.

I was eight years old when I first felt England invade me,
Bobby Sands bled from a mural on a once ordinary house,
men who never went to Ireland clinked tankards in glee.

I was twenty-one years old when I first felt Ireland,
a horse with a severed rope chewed roses on Dundrum Road,
nobody was bothered, *it was bothering nobody*.

I was twenty-one when I first felt England in Dublin.
a stag night from London turned Garda blue and ugly
it was the end of the troubles yet cockney lads invaded us.

43ᴿᴰ BIRTHDAY

> *Suicide is the single biggest killer of men aged under 45 in the UK. In 2015, 75% of all UK suicides were male.*
> — CalmZone

Unearthing you is a disturbed treasure,
that last glass of red grainy as a *Truprint* sunset
an immaculate house and your note of broken maps to why.

To say your name is to bring you home in a wooden birdhouse.
Each time I see our mother blow you out in Rothmans
she remembers your incense, the birth and still deaths.

To say your name is to admit you go to God grey and cold.
Each time I see our father he is a cradle of bone
there are holes instead of eyes, tomb dark.

Unearthing you is the colour of Facebook blues and reds,
ninety-four comments that say nothing and everything,
sixty-three emoticons weep at a coffin of pixels.

BAGHDAD ZOO
After Leanne Bridgewater

There was a place in the municipal cosmos
where bomb craters became bird baths
and garlands of foxes slept in tyres.

At Baghdad Zoo you could hear music in a tiger's eye
you could roam the Serengeti there
as far away as Babylon and Mars.

A sniper made an exploding rainbow
he shot a macaw confused on the wire
nothing personal just war and boredom.

At Baghdad Zoo a wolf could have left its enclosure
he thought the moon had given up on him
jailed in ribs the heart packs up like a market watch.

It is easy to herd kept animals back to where they belong,
they are nothing but eyes floating like dead planets
here in the cosmos of Iraq it is the end of worlds.

SREBRENICA MASSACRE

For the 8000+ Muslims massacred in 1994

I had to work harder to learn about you,
it's as if you were killed twice-over
first by gun then by side column.
If only you were fashionable
then I could find you
share you, like you
add emoticons
Srebrenica.

To find the doves we must look for crows;
the smiling architect shaking hands,
peacekeepers overrun by minions.
Imagine Father and son lined up
Twin towers over the ground
two bullets smashing skulls
bone matter, *don't matter* —
page nine of a paper
known for a day.
If only you, were
fashionable.

THE MATHEMATICS OF PEACE

Picture an old man
with numbers on his arm
shuddering by burst gas pipes.
I think he would see the gassing of my child
and help me,
I think we could be friends,
press each other's wounds.

Picture a sea of children,
eyes pitted like Palestinian olives
picture them being dragged by the legs to fists,
six numbers on arms add to nothing.

If I left my house,
where would I go and who would take me?
My children are walking into the sea wanting to die.
This is the sum of forced displacement.

A KOREAN SOLDIER IS BLOWN IN HALF
After "Massacre in Korea" by Pablo Picasso, 1951

Think of her not as the enemy
lowering like a pail to her legs.
Think of her body as north and south,
the mind and eyes its northernmost point
watching the south part of her drift like continents.

Had I have been born more southerly ninety years ago
somewhere near a prohibited sea by the bony shale
would a stork hand me a white feather shrieking?
Would it know of what awaits in the widow-lands?
I think I may be someone different, *we'll never know.*

A Korean soldier is blown in half, *walk past her.*
Go to the DMZ and draw the line in boiling tar,
use the same brush for friends and constant enemies.
Laugh at how crazy they seem with their daft ways.
Hate them for eating dogs and don't let sleeping dogs lie.

ASTRONAUTS

For Aylan Kurdi

I want to stay here in paradise and vote for bream and rice as children shoot each other safely dying like pretend refugees. I want to raise the runt that was tied to the leash of a mongrel and walk it through the ferns and stare south to my homeland and pray. I want to tell my nephew that his mother and Father were astronauts of water and live floating among the stars that whales blow out to the sky.

Oh, my beautiful friends I have had to vote for many things that would break your red little ships and sink them in your chests. I have had to vote to leave my daughter and place my faith in driftwood. I want to stay here in paradise and watch my brother's boy dream and tell him that sea monsters do not yell in Arabic to be saved.

I want to open this locket and tell my wife that the olives here are bitter and how Greek widows stand on towels to collect them for the women. I want to vote for water tomorrow and ask Jurgen why he wears a Leicester top when last year he supported United. I want you to hear how children here pass a football, my turn, your turn, my turn your turn, my turn, my turn my turn, my turn.

They are voting which players they want on their side. They are playing for this camp; they are playing to be children. They are making up the rules.

THE NAGASAKI ELDER

V. PRESS (2017)

THE LAST FARE COLLECTOR OF HIROSHIMA

They found her fingers in a jelly of yen
her skin one with the standard issue fare bag
a dove in a sen of silver to go to the mountains oh if only she went.

I have read of a woman who cooled her burns with figs and persimmon
she pared away old skin for years the finest paper it was
writing its kanji into the papyrus sky I wish I knew her.

In the ritual of tea-making I learnt how to sip from a widow's eyes and
learn that some stories are like Hiroshima streetcars
they always arrive on time then the hour takes them.

They found her fables in the evening crow
hopping by the river it is time to hear how atoms sound
when another survivor dies their story sinks at the shore of their eyes.

I have read of a god-fearing woman who feared man so much more
she sliced a cucumber each night for years to cool her skin
and hate had left her years ago with five generations of

Fisherman
    horse-breaker
        cleaner
            librarian
                Mother
                    Father
                        Sister
                            fare-collector.

PEARL HARBOUR
After Jacques Gaucheron

In Hiroshima, there are many pearl harbours
burning in waters of survivor's eyes and I
have watched these oysters prise open through grief —
a pale glaucoma where the photographed dot
explodes *that day* in the grief-linished pupils.

In Hiroshima, there were many boats on fire
floating in the six rivers like Viking burials,
thousands of rags anchored to the old place
from limbs caught on trees rigor mortis —
did they never want to leave this city of water and fire?

In Hiroshima, they harvest pearls in the inland sea
and some use these spent shells for soup bowls
or ashtrays, but some hold the tale to their ears
and hear the dead whispering to those who drank them —
"I am a shadow that once cast a boy, hiding in the open"

THE NAGASAKI ELDER

Her first son was silent
as if refusing to weep from that beautiful slum —
the still yellow flower of Nagasaki took nine months to bloom.

Her first kiss was black rain
writing tragic symphonies on song-sheet glass;
her father is the boogeyman haunted by his face from slithers.

Her first period was jelly.
The shift Mothers came trained to hold survivors,
do not say a word to the handsome doctor who writes for your blood.

Her first revolution was spinning a potter's wheel anti clockwise;
re-shaping her family with Nagasaki clay, she said —
this is how water should feel.

GREEN TOMATO

Look at those boats of bone in rivers —
last night their eyes were lighthouses
shining blue and brown in natural darkness.

Look at that shape ripped apart like rags —
the pinafore spoke what sex it was;
she died with a green tomato punctured on red lips.

Look at that crucifix smelted to *its* skin —
her lifeline blew in the Fahrenheit wind;
three children they read with a long and healthy life.

Look at all these unripe tomatoes in mouths —
they died the moment they sucked the juice,
made another mountain on school playgrounds.

BLACK RAIN

For Yumiko

You were the sun
that stole a rainbow
from arcs of Hiroshima bridges,
and how you chose your colours.
First, magnesium reds twined like blood in water,
then you stole blue and brown from eyes of children,
but black is what you wanted the most, a certain shade.

So, you mixed the colours
with burning hair and wind,
unshackled the shadows free from all their flesh,
but they wept in the blood-drenched dusk
and the only way to return to Hiroshima
was to weep as black rain to where they had risen,
nourishing the scorched tundra in eggshell raindrops
until they exploded as oleanders.

PURPLE CHALK

Years after the bomb startled water,
koi engulfed the egg-flecked banks
spawning shockwaves of life.

Years after the ill star was born,
shy women revealed themselves
to men who took their blood and husbands.

Months after the first silent births,
a mother took her unnamed life
and then her soul in a whispering river.

Weeks after, this girl with the handprint face
explained she was counting to ten, then a flash
printed hide and seek on her face.

Days after, a boy wrote his name in purple chalk —
his yo-yoing eyes spilled across his frame;
they washed his feet before he died.

Before he died, he asked *why me?*
The boy on the human bonfire
returned to water with koi.

TO FEED A NAGASAKI STARLING

She said don't go to the shadows without water —
I have tried to erase him for sixty-four years
and my wrists are tired;
I have scrubbed the darkness of my son
so he could be buried at last in sunlight.

Don't go to my son without removing your shoes —
I have tried to bathe him with prayers and carbolic
but he only gets blacker;
I have lived for ninety-nine years
and starlings are beginning to land by my feet.

Don't wind the paralysed clock,
it is rebuilding the world with seared hands –
I have tried to turn back time
but God will not allow it in Nagasaki;
I had tried to make another child but gave birth to pink curd.

Don't tell them my name,
and look me in the face when you see him —
I have tried to understand
why ink is only spilled by vaporised kin;
I have tried to write a haiku
for the willow which strokes my son.

Don't disturb my son
when the raven plays in the shape of his spectre —
I have tried to shoo it away and it quarrels with my broomstick;
I have tried to tell my son that he was ten yards from living.

I have tried to feed a Nagasaki starling
when it drank the black rain;
I have tried to get it to sing so this wraith could be comforted –
don't disturb my grave and desecrate me
with twitching shadows.

FAT MAN

> *You ask what is our aim? I can answer in one word. It is victory. Victory at all costs. Victory in spite of all terrors. Victory however long and hard the road may be, for without victory there is no survival.*
> — Winston Churchill

Oh, ribbon weaver
what did you weave in the war room
for Coventry?

Fine sky-blue yarns,
fat Havana halos, the prophetic ligature
for stained black saints.

Oh, war shepherd
the mauling wolves embed our moon,
torn against our spire.

Toe tags queue for names —
a child they thought was a beam
was younger than your brandy.

Oh, ribbon weaver
what will you weave for Dresden
from Coventry's stone elbows?

The Nagasaki bastard
they named after you
whistled like a soldier,

bloomed for the lotus flower,
your carbonised legacy.
Fat Man, fire, criminal.

SKETCHING OF AN ATOMIC HORSE

> *Why did the ants crawl back into the house just before the atom bomb was dropped? Did they know of what was to come?"*
> — *Coventry School Student upon seeing* 'Barefoot Gen'

In pastures of blank white pages
someone captured a nag through graphite
rubbing its lead mane in the dropped stars' corona.

Pencil on page is a cruel stable:
a nag lapping troughs of her wounds,
the hurled tongue green from ghosts of grass.

There is no shame in falling twice —
a neigh of hot hail stampedes the thoroughbred;
art pulls the drowned foal from eyes.

THE FERRYMAN

I often think of that unnamed road in Nagasaki
where the 'o' of her breast remained untouched by fire
as her daughter suckled to live through *Fat Man's* crucible.

I often think of the man who found them as Pompeii ornaments
standing there knowing he would soon pay Charon at the shore,
as he drifted away from *Sake* and swords born of fire and water.

I often think of Nagasaki Mothers as sheets for their babies.
We are going to sleep in a manger of weird flames,
death will display us like screaming white logs.

I often think of those things the bomb breathed upwards —
tatami mats and door knobs found high in mountains,
dentures welded to the bones of a charred umbrella.

I choose to forget the image that made Charon weep —
East of the river *Ota* when he suckled at the banks,
he saw a manger of skulls weeping crayfish.

THE ART OF WAR (I)

The old Hiroshima trees in autumn scratch the ill wind till it bleeds in time for spring when the dead each blow a petal and their fragrant inferno engulfs a man coughing blossoms of blood from weak boughs of bone, but he is a strong root. He told me when spring leaves Hiroshima, all that remains of trees are fingers of the dead, holding birds that swept across sky like ashes, throwing their urn of shrieks to a scarlet sun hurling the war of blood inside. Every year, the cherry blossoms get redder and a zephyr sighs as they fall. The rivers in every petal are souls who drank the wrong rain; they are louder each year for the shadows that are lighter, spilled like quill pots of unwritten lives. Hiroshima streets are a Pollock canvas. From shockwaves of pure monsoon rain, the drip-drop dragonflies brush watercolours on grave-grey rivers and dusk-fall are an easel, yet the saddest artist twice drew a black orchid on a blue face.

A PARK NEAR CHERNOBYL
After Mario Petrucci

Sons hung in lockets blinking from trees.
Pounding in the stricken heart,
a father sieved dust for his daughters.

Tanoy's collapsed the legs of mothers
echoing names of rush buried men
their blue bodies still as the moon's pale sea.

Outside, the fairground grew sick.
A cello exchanged Mozart for bread,
snails mocked the moored dodgems.

Stiff men stapled names of the dead.
Mothers flung God to ground
retrieving photographs of sellotaped sons.

Picture the unused Ferris wheel —
caged within its silence,
spent with sun's rusted rouble.

The cats that cleaned themselves
died en route to privacy;
they purred through sonar blips.

In veiled maternity wards
babes bloomed flower-heads —
their tongues were anthers.

HOW TO SURVIVE A NUCLEAR WINTER

> *The unleashed power of the atom has changed everything save our modes of thinking and we thus drift toward unparalleled catastrophe.*
> — Albert Einstein

Beneath the welt of a nuclear moon,
we'll meet in government shelters,
 sing merry cockney songs in subways foggy with stench;
help will come in books of flames.

 All the cars are gunmetal grey;
we harvest screen-wash for wounds.
At night, marauders make smog from bodies in acres of lye –
they wheel the meat to the ice rink.

We catch crows to feed them turnips; if they live, we eat them.
At night, we collect hair from Kylie's comb;
it stops her child from bawling.

In meagre hours of daylight,
 we smash mirrors to keep us pretty.
 Kylie went mad there, took her own life
by shouting rebel poems to child lieutenants.

We do not go by days but by schedules, and they can kill you.
Last week we saw sun for the first time in weeks;
 they shot six people roaming in wonderment.

The next time moon burns through ragged fallout,
I'll loiter on the rubble of my house,
yelling war poems by Edith Sitwell,
waiting for haggard children –
the jurors of russet knives.

MARGARET THATCHER'S MUSEUM

HESTERGLOCK PRESS (2015)

KIM KARDASHIAN BROKE THE INTERNET

From white flowers of hoarfrost
you watch cinders of starlings
turn pages of hymnbook sky and
throw your sister into the moon

And all the forest mourns her
a crow leaves a tantrum from the spire
a fox spills the guts of a bin bag
a badger is culled by a hearse.

You say all mother's become altars
the minute they bury their children
a different water breaks like a sigil.

And the whole town lines Main Street,
a child ties lilies to the lampposts stalk
a man takes a selfie looking broken in Gucci
and Kim Kardashian broke the internet.

FERRIES

Ferries across Hillsborough
were rivers of driftwood hoardings,
severed wavelets of siren blue
surfaced on drowned chests.

The doorways of leppings lane
housed dilated occupants
a theft of borrowed belongings
like fronds in flaccid liver birds.

Assess the foundations
a girl carried once in her Ma
carried twice to rest on her Da,
crumbling on raised earth.

There's a pea that crushed the whistles throat,
a silence freed from working class memorials
they dug for decades with shards of an hourglass
unearthing the vital minutes.

THE COLD WAR

After shifts we turned beds of an overgrown paddock,
cut silence with stones we lobbed at factory cats and
Mum stared at Dad staring where his dad knelt in Spring.

After shifts I watched my dad take deep breaths by the gate,
looking for the son in himself so he could play as sky broke,
and he broke, with half price bread that smelt of turmeric.

After shifts, Jagdish stopped moaning how black he felt
when Dad patted snowmen black till his hands burnt
walking into headlights like a poor man's James Dean.

After shifts a klaxon shot birds over our rooftops and we drank
those cups of grass where redstarts sang the lyric of factories from.
One night the snow stopped but the song carried on till dawn.

After shifts I wanted to be like my dad and bend things with fire
but something made the snowman collapse into itself whilst smiling,
it was a bit like all of us that winter in nineteen eighty-two.

NIGEL FARAGE STREET

> *I think secretly she would have cheered him on. I think he voices a lot of her prejudices*
> — Jonathan Aitken, Former Conservative MP

Walk with me down Nigel Farage Street
and let's pound the street like a fascists flag.
We'll pass the bunting of a slaughtered pig
then you will look offended and I'll speak
token British things to make you feel better like
Mum said you're lovely for an Indian and still
lovely when I said you're Pakistani.

Walk with me through minarets of snow and
we'll worship the sunset on Imperial Road then
place a bet at the bookies where hope falls with
the underdog but we'll both lose together
skulking off with our winnings of free reggae
past Jagienka's house muralled in street art,
these streets bleed to life each night you said.

THE OTHER IRON LADY

I was the song swaddled from your womb and
   you said my heart felt like rain, a feint whisper
of your Da when he gave you away in a hired veil.

I was the half world you half made and carried
   to young wives' club where women knitted limbs
of blue and pink, just to be on the safe side.

I was the little monster who scared you in the last month
   when I hadn't kicked you for soup and arctic roll that
had to be from *Bejam* and rush-bought from my Da.

I was the unnamed flame pulsing in the night sky
   filling cracks of hands that punched pistons
and a bloke down the road who swore at me Ma.

I was the son of a woman who spelt big words wrong
   yet did little things right, who knew the dialect of love
was the great unsaid till it had to be, said

I was the son of a man who drank beer but displayed wine
   in spray oak cabinets so people thought us posh
till Ma said *shit* and *sorry* and *take me as you find me.*

I was the son of an unremarkable woman
   who wanted to be clever but a mother more,
yeah; I was the son of a song never heard.

THE YEAR I LOVED ENGLAND

PIGHOG PUBLISHING (2014)

THE DREAMER OF SAMUEL VALE HOUSE

We sat by kerb trees denied of Autumn.
Watched the black and decker blossom that
brushed the eight fourteen to Courtaulds.

Tonight, I'll tune into rain and blackbird aerials
make pictures from Air India clouds
watch magpies scrape song from tyre track birds.

With grade two bricks scrumped from the gatehouse
I'll watch bored kids re-open the factory
admire their work where there is none.

Tonight, I'll walk you home to the sky
to floor thirty-six we'll look down on everyone
and wish upon stars of a 747.

Everyone is leaving here or arrived from a tent,
I have googled the earth and am tired of paradise
This city is home, I am its key and broken door.

COVENTRY STREET

This city lost another street today
a baker threw his thumbprints to birds,
legs of lamb were walked to a skip.

This street was named after a watchmaker,
his hands stroke the bell towers face
pigeons swoop for burgers there.

This city progressed today,
a busker buried his symphonies
walked headless to Starbucks.

My city lost its voice today,
in its stone-grey throat
a song was soulless.

THE YEAR I LOVED ENGLAND

A part of you was human in that rush hour
when brake-lights gouged their abscess of dead dreams.

I was asleep in the timed warmth of strike year,
factory kids were gaps in milk crates by classrooms.

In the years of your longest days I never went without a dad,
we only moaned as spitfires down keep out hills.

A part of me was adult when they broke you that Friday,
the down on your arms came from my pocket money.

In the year I loved England you plucked blackthorns from my hand,
rubbed away down from the nettle's sting.

In the year I loved England a man left the house
and returned unmade from the smokeless factory.

In the year I loved England my dad lost his dad,
found an orphan grey in the glass.

I was awake when you should have been sleeping,
you timed your grief into your father's shirt.

There is a poem stuffed in sad black suits,
for father's we bury and resurrect,
from clothes that wear us with yesterday's sweat.

THE BURNING OF NUMBER EIGHT'S WHEELIE BIN

Maybe it was that Tuesday, her yapping handbag,
a faux leather finger stiff to the natives.

The Waitrose van on a dropped kerb driveway
where offending leylandii blocked patriotic tenements.

Maybe it was that Friday when Iqbal knocked her door
with rainbows of Lahore in tin foil cartons,

showed off his Audi, took her for a spin,
where windows change to plywood at the mosque.

Boys in makeshift burkas sprayed white nigga with a typo,
they ran with paint staining the streets.

Last Tuesday the ginnell shone gold from her wheelie bin.
They found bones of lamb dopiaza and a Pekinese.

THE LITTLE THINGS DESTROY US

When I was a son
you closed with the factories,
broke things to fix them.

You grew a moustache,
wore unemployed clothes,
caged your world in a shed.

That black leg Easter you wept,
Thatcher glided in a Daimler,
like spit on union coats.

In the blue asbestos sleet
you groaned with embroidered steel,
hocking slush in shiny basins.

The Christmas Nissan cancelled
you wrapped the road in fumes,
tore through sleet with a grimace.

I was your son a long time ago,
when I raced to the gate
of your Kawasaki symphony.

Childhood was an itchy caravan
on a site full of white folk
wrestling with wind breakers.

Childhood was a magic trick,
it vanished with the work,
sometime in the eighties.

That day I ran into blackthorns
you plucked them out like feathers,
the plume of your pipe calmed me.

The little things destroy us,
anchors to childhood are heavy,
sometimes they drown us.

FAUN

Here come the sons of Adam,
half-human fauns conjoined,
bones of a bagpipe's lament.

Here come the fathers of war,
heads bowed with bucket flowers,
amputated like benefits.

Here come three lions roaring on cloth,
laid to rest on a stone table,
squeaking on rope over Whitehall Narnia.

Here come the true flags,
furred clothes wearing wardrobes,
the last battle *lost.*

Here come the real hymns for God,
a lifetime of two-minute silences,
bugles turning fauns to stone.

LOGO

In the twice murdered park
they cordoned off frost,
diggers stabbed the paddling pool.

In hypodermic dew
tarmac clung to a see-saw,
a robin bloodied the bough.

Come April where blossom used to fall,
we'll drink cappuccino, get caught in moments
like carrier bags on bus level trees.

Come April we can queue outside Primark,
I'll buy me a new me
on the playground I discovered myself.

Come March I shall walk to the swings,
push the seat where fathers made childhoods
and gob the way Darren did.

Come March I'll peel paint from the carousel,
reveal the name of a lay student
who necked wine and a teacher's tongue.

Come March sky is a logo.

VERMIN
   For Denise Taylor

A fox came to Powell Estate,
sipped sky from my bird-table.
We exchanged territories.

Ablaze in mist she glided to leftovers.
Cities have eaten the forest,
her snout sews the green man's ghost.

Vermin and baby made front pages.
I read in a side column not long ago
they were shooting dogs in Rwanda.

THE SHELF STACKER

On riot black bricks
a welder sprayed the lie
washed away by unnoticed youths
doing their time in high vis.

Sunset is chained to a swing,
its mural bled in the playground
with fists of a jobseeker,
searching the works of rage.

Our streets gleam gold in the rain,
derelict shops are cold beds of youth
clutching their stomachs,
like cheap handbags.

Downtown the streets are cleaned for trade,
diamonds of a cobbler's window brushed into bags,
a youth wears his preacher's label,
the welder forced to stack shelves.

THE DREADED BOY

PIGHOG PUBLISHING (2011)

MEDUSA

The mouth of the aircraft swallowed her husband,
brought back Medusa.

When they make love, he looks away,
his eyes never left her before.

She planned to celebrate his homecoming,
he disappears at gatherings.

The day he returned, his dog was so excited
its heart packed up.

He embedded a razor blade in soap
washed himself and wept.

She declared her love would never die
he raised a fist and she kissed it.

His little brother asked to see his medals,
he took him to a friend's grave.

He was hailed a hero in the paper
and stoked the furnace with it.

His wife wants to try for a baby,
he packed his bags for war.

THE SCENT OF A SON

Three lions roar through cirrhus
dens of silica await them.
Triumphant mouths of brass
fill frown lines with tears.
Soon they will shoot sky
and reload the soil.

Our skies are pall bearers.
Aeroplanes writing wisps of men,
moaning high over Darlington,
landing in a loved one's throat.
In London ministers argue expenses
in York a father fills carrier bag
walking the scent of his son to Oxfam.

PENDANT

On bleak dunes
of greying youth
snow laid a wrinkled wreath.

Names somersault from mouths
their winter breaths
are informers.

Screams of war have no accent,
and scarlet rags
of bullets shall wear them.

No-man's-land is a room
with a face in a door handle
that hurts too much to turn.

The pendant sun shall wear their faces,
untouched like medals
in locked shrines.

EGGS

In Gaza the swallows are chirping from bullet holes.
They make their nests with jettison —
cardboard, cotton, human hair.

Someone painted grenades for the children,
to glimmer in primary colours
by limbs of a road refugees made.

Somewhere, hens are hatching eggs,
painting rainbows with ring-pulls.
The trees sprawl out to stars like Hannukia's.

Candles glow out from the heavens
flickering from a child's breath
their fingers charred like tapers.

THE QUIET NIGHTS OF WAR

In the Hollywood hills of human remains
she fanned herself with a burnt Quran
to wear his breath of jasmine and cordite.

Every night she tucks him into bed
cupping sandbanks with saliva,
the barren earth is with child.

A map of their village burned in the fire,
etched on an elder's back
wolves left tusks of his grimacing spine.

Orphans trekked to a cave
where martyrs groomed their grief,
they stared through white men in white cars.

Every night her war passes them by,
a convoy rolls rocks from his grave
she puts them back one by one.

DIAMONDS

After Dr Karen Woo

He stroked her hair from a bobby pin.
His throat swelled like the Nuristan River,
for a smile that shaded only once,
from souks of a gun.

They confirmed her surname phonetically,
three letters were all it took
to lock away the world,
open a wardrobe and breathe her in.

He is the marble tide's fiancé
dressing the love of his life
in gossamer frocks of urn.
She smashed into diamonds.

MY FATHER'S EYES WERE BLUE

HEAVENTREE PRESS (2009)

FOXGLOVES

In the stillness of wheat-packed fields
I walked into skies the colour of barley
chased the yolky orb
before it hatched silver.
Vixens hung on wire
bowing to their own exposed guts
free at last from the baying hounds,
the genteel savages unleashed.

The sky seemed appropriate,
bloodied and still
numbed by eerie solitude.
I fell by jellied foxgloves,
broken like oaks
at the death of my childhood

THE SPIDER AND THE WIFE

From your lips to mine
you weaved silk in cotton
and a spider crawled
on akimbo shadows.

Every lie was a strand
perfectly formed;
usually on weekends
when guilt forced your lips
on the back of my neck
by the digital flicker –
where the minutes crept
like forgotten heroes.

You screamed out my name
yet thought of his,
your web caught me
and I let you dine on my insides
in a jewel of salt.

I thought of his drooling jaw
Curdling the breasts that fed our son.
My wife once sang beautifully o
of mockingbirds she'd bring
but then brought a spider and a stepdad
who left when the webs finished.

THE COPPER MAN

Somewhere on Mayfair pavements,
amongst the flocking drones,
a jelly-necked vagrant
lay dead on sodden cardboard,
dressed in Versace shadows
and coppers they flicked.

His Labrador licked him,
changing from gold to blue,
barking and biting at neon reapers
who took away his master,
muzzling his grief.

Embedded in the vagrants palm
Was a medal from King George.
The pauper box is planed.
Let's just bury him,
Shrapnel for our conscience,
And I'm late for my meeting

ACKNOWLEDGEMENTS

I would like to thank the editors of the following publications where these poems first appeared:
Magma, Envoi, Poetry International (Europe), *The Journal of The Wilfred Owen Association, Warscapes, International Times, Under the radar, Peace Insight, Lacuna Magazine* (Warwick University Human Rights), *National Army Poetry Competition 2018 Prize-winners' Anthology, The Wilfred Owen Story, Voicing Suicide Anthology* (Ekstasis Press & Asylum Magazine), *Ink Sweat & Tears, International Times, The Twin Project, Snakeskin, Picaroon, Amaryllis, Until the stars burn out, Riggwelter Journal, Proletarian Poetry, Dark River Literary Journal, Penance, I am not a silent poet, Fresh Air Magazine, The Curly Mind, The Broken Bugle, Interrogative Papers, Radon Journal, Stand.*

Other notable publications & features:
CND UK Hiroshima & Nagasaki Exhibition (2022)
Quakers UK
University College London
National Army Poetry Competition 2018: *Writing Armistice.* (Winner of the Museum of Military Medicine Category for "*A Black Nurse Tends to Wounds*".)
Dresden Orchestra (Musical compositions of Inferno and other poems performed at the Frauenkirche, Dresden).
Enola Gay is a donated peace education resource for Quakers Peace Education UK and CND Peace Education UK and was included in a Quakers UK Peace Podcast discussion about modern conflict and Peace Education resources in January 2018.
A black nurse tends to wounds was read and recorded in the ruins of Coventry Cathedral for Armistice on 11/11/2018.

Several Hiroshima and Nagasaki poems have been taught by Professor R Klein at poetry workshop classes in Hiroshima and performed for CND, Coventry Cathedral and Positive Images Festival.

With gratitude to Aaron Kent and the team at Broken Sleep for producing this book and for being a lantern for poetry that illuminates the human darkness in the world so we can pay witness. And with gratitude to all the peace education leaders for their support of me over the years mot notably John Hartley, Hideko Okamoto, Prof R. Klein Rainer Barczaitis, David Fish, Isabel Cartwright, Elllis Brookes and Hans Svennnevig,

LAY OUT YOUR UNREST